Chris Jericho's rivalry with AJ Styles was one of the high points of 2016. Jericho's defeat of Styles at *WrestleMania* marked his first victory at the Show of Shows since 2010.

At *SummerSlam*, Finn Bálor unleashed the Demon King on Seth Rollins to become the first-ever WWE Universal Champion. Bálor, Rollins and Kevin Owens are the only Superstars to have held the NXT title and a WWE world championship.

BEST OF WWE 2016

THE MATCHES, SUPERSTARS AND SHAKEUPS THAT LEFT THE WWE UNIVERSE IN AWE.

08
BEST OF RAW
In 2016, the flagship show of WWE brought fans to their feet time and again.

28
BEST OF SMACKDOWN
The Blue Brand was host to thrilling bouts and explosive Superstars all year.

54
BEST OF NXT
Not to be outdone by the main roster, the Superstars of tomorrow made big waves in 2016.

72
BEST OF THE BEST
Some events and competitors made such an impact this year, they belong in their own elite class.

John Cena looks on, stunned, as Big Cass turns Enzo Amore into a flying weapon against The Club at *Battleground*. The daring move helped lead to victory at the event.

BEST OF RAW

IN 2016, WWE'S MONDAY NIGHTS WERE ALL ABOUT STUNNING DEBUTS, BOUNDARY-BREAKING WOMEN AND UNEXPECTED COMEBACKS. HERE ARE SOME OF THE STANDOUTS.

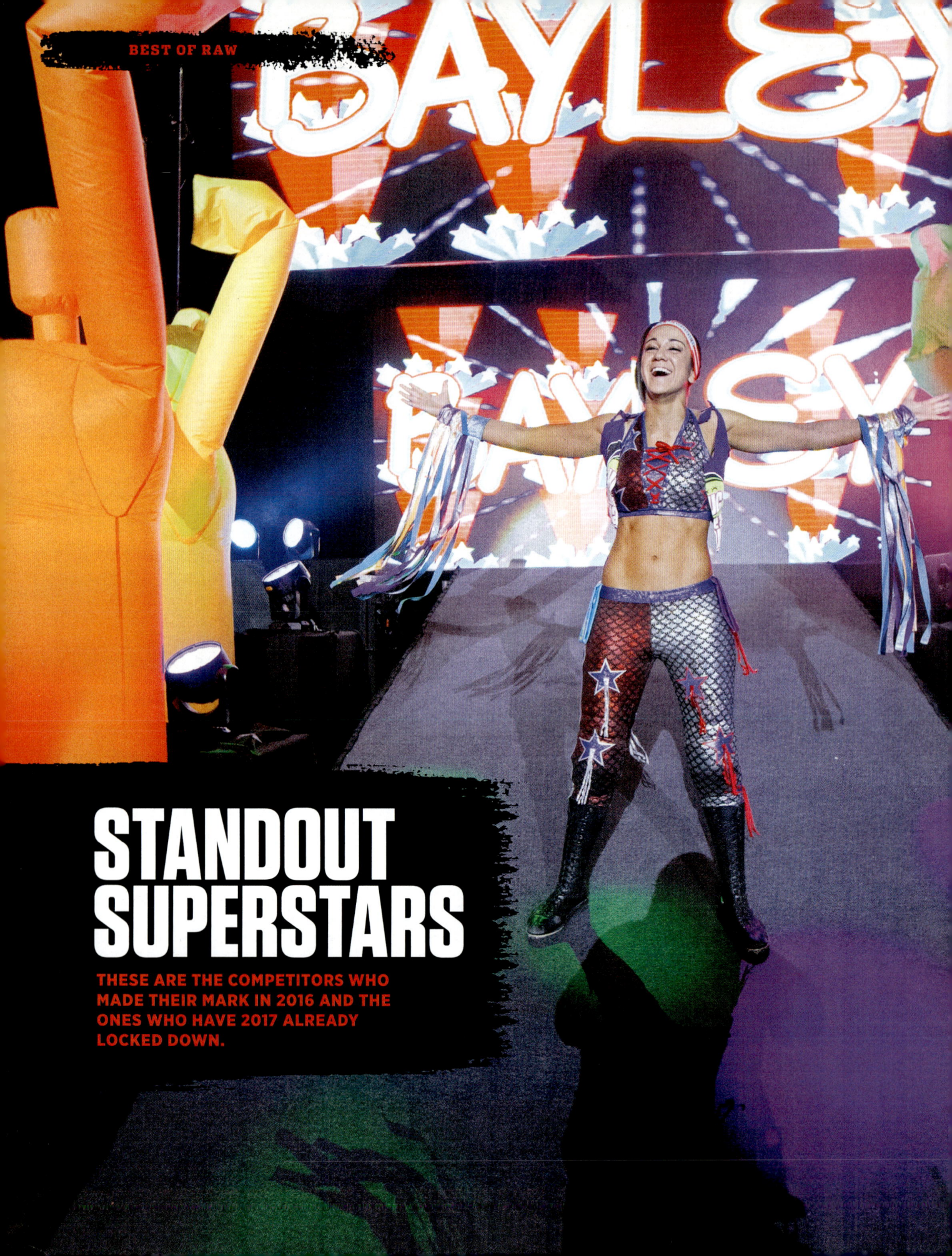

BEST OF RAW

STANDOUT SUPERSTARS

THESE ARE THE COMPETITORS WHO MADE THEIR MARK IN 2016 AND THE ONES WHO HAVE 2017 ALREADY LOCKED DOWN.

BAYLEY
MOST HUGGABLE

A star in *NXT*, Bayley made waves in 2015 when she competed against Sasha Banks in the first-ever women's Iron Man match at *NXT TakeOver: Respect*, setting a new standard for female competition in WWE. Bayley managed to defeat Banks three falls to two, retaining the Women's title and proving she had what it took to make the leap to the main roster. Finally, the day after *SummerSlam* 2016, the WWE Universe at large got the chance to meet Bayley when she was hand-selected by Mick Foley to come to *Raw*. With her feisty, fun-loving personality and penchant for side-ponytails, Bayley quickly became a fan favorite. And her hard-hitting technical style in the ring made her the bane of female competitors across the roster. She immediately went after reigning Women's Champion Charlotte, and, while she hasn't yet claimed the gold, her stunning run in *NXT* proves Bayley's bouts in the big leagues are just getting started.

BROCK LESNAR
LEAST HUGGABLE

When Lesnar returned to WWE in 2012, speculation ran rampant as to the nature of his intentions. Was this a one-off? A cash grab? A chance to reset his post-2004 legacy? In the last four years, the first two notions have been laid to rest. Lesnar wasn't back just to show up on *Raw*, F5 a couple of Superstars and leave. He was in it for the long haul. And his legacy? Well, you tell us. Lesnar has left a swath of broken Superstars in his wake since returning, and he demolished The Undertaker's *WrestleMania* streak in 2014. In 2016, Lesnar went back on the warpath, defeating Dean Ambrose in a No Holds Barred Street Fight at *WrestleMania* and facing off against Randy Orton at *SummerSlam* in a bout that saw the Viper go down by TKO. He then nailed Shane McMahon with an F5 for good measure. But his greatest challenge came toward the end of the year when, in a completely unexpected turn of events, Goldberg returned to WWE to challenge Lesnar to a match at *Survivor Series*. This is the grudge match fans have been waiting for since 2004 when Goldberg defeated Lesnar in a match that has been seen as an ignominious end to their first runs in WWE. But, whether it's a grudge match, street fight or streak-threatening *WrestleMania* match, Lesnar has proven that, when he's in the ring, he's in his element. And everyone else? They're in trouble.

BEST OF RAW

STANDOUT SUPERSTARS

TJ PERKINS
MOST GEEKTASTIC ENTRANCE

Is it possible to be both retro and current at the same time? Somehow TJ's video game-inspired entrance manages to pull it off. Whether you're a hardcore gamer or don't know a double jump from a double down, it's hard not to get amped when TJ hits Max Health and bursts down the ramp.

SETH ROLLINS
THE "WE HATE HIM/LOVE HIM" AWARD

In 2014, Seth Rollins broke our hearts when he destroyed the Shield. But he won us back over after he was brutally Pedigreed by Triple H, allowing Kevin Owens to become Universal Champion. After that, Rollins waged a one-man war on The Authority, using every trick he learned after two years on the inside. Although he hasn't yet toppled Owens to claim the gold, we know The Architect won't stop until he's achieved his goals. Welcome back, Seth. All is forgiven. For now.

BRAUN STROWMAN
BEST IMPRESSION OF A MOUNTAIN

The former Wyatt acolyte is now on his own and is less a WWE Superstar and more a terrifying force of nature. After being drafted to *Raw*, Strowman began mowing through the competition with the fury of an M1 Abrams tank. As of press time, he remains undefeated on *Raw*, and we can't imagine who could possibly arise to reduce Strowman to rubble.

THE LIST OF JERICHO
BEST SUPERSTAR (WHO ISN'T A SUPERSTAR)

A relative latecomer to the WWE scene in 2016, Chris Jericho's "List of Jericho," an ever-expanding roster of Superstars that grind his gears, has become the one place you don't want to end up. But, for the WWE Universe, nothing is more entertaining than hearing Jericho intone to an unlucky competitor, "You just made the list!"

BEST OF RAW
TOP TAG TEAMS

THE NEW DAY
BEST TAG TEAM AGAINST ALL ODDS

For two years now, The New Day have bucked the odds and flown in the face of convention. And, in the process, completely reinvented what it means to be a WWE tag team. When they first debuted, no one believed they'd last. They were too loud, too abrasive, too different and seemingly obsessed with the word "booty." But The New Day soldiered on and now stand as the longest-reigning champs in the history of the *Raw* tag titles, clocking in at more than a year. The question is no longer will someone beat them for their titles. The question is, do we want that to happen?

ENZO & BIG CASS
REALEST TAG TEAM IN ANY ROOM

With Enzo Amore, every word out of his mouth is a quotable catchphrase, and (say it with us) "You can't teach that!" When paired up with Big Cass, the muscle to back up the mouth, they form a tag team that's a fusion of quick wit and quicker moves. While they haven't yet ascended to the heights of other teams in the division, they've provided no shortage of entertainment and always managed to keep it real. How you doin'?

LUKE GALLOWS & KARL ANDERSON
MOST LIKELY TO BE SUED FOR MALPRACTICE

We're not sure where Gallows and Anderson received their medical degrees, but it doesn't seem like they're adhering to the oath of "First Do No Harm." Quite the opposite, in fact. While warning the WWE roster of the dangers of "ringpostitis," they conveniently gloss over the fact that they're responsible for the majority of outbreaks!

WWE THE BEST OF 2016 **15**

BEST OF RAW
MIC DROPS

MOST CLEVERLY PAINFUL INSULT

THE CERTIFIED G WAS NOT INTERESTED IN DRINKING IN THE GIFT OF JERICHO....

"Jericho, listening to you speak, time passes like a kidney stone."
—Enzo Amore, cutting down Chris Jericho on *Raw*, 8/1/16

WORDS WE'VE WAITED TOO LONG TO HEAR

12 YEARS, TO BE EXACT

"Brock Lesnar, you're not just next, you're last!"
—Goldberg, calling out The Beast on *Raw*, 10/17/16

BEST OF RAW
RIVETING RIVALRIES

KEVIN OWENS VS. SAMI ZAYN
WORST BEST FRIEND AWARD

While he may be Chris Jericho's best friend now, Kevin Owens has an ugly history of betraying his buddies. After years of battling together around the world, in basements and back alleys as they struggled to the top, Kevin Owens and Sami Zayn seemed to always have each others' backs. That all changed in December of 2014 at *NXT TakeOver: R Evolution*, when Owens powerbombed Sami onto the ring apron shortly after Zayn's winning of the *NXT* title. That heinous betrayal sparked a bitter rivalry that continued when Zayn dashed Owens's hopes of winning the 2016 Royal Rumble match. The two ex-chums continued to work out their differences in a series of grudge matches, ending at *Battleground*, when Owens was defeated by Zayn. While these good friends did seem to make better enemies, we hope 2017 sees these former besties back on the same side.

ROMAN REIGNS VS. RUSEV
WORST BEST MAN AWARD

As Rusev and Lana attempted to celebrate their nuptials, Roman Reigns decided to play both wedding crasher and best man, giving a spur-of-the-moment toast that didn't so much honor the bride and groom as viciously insult them. The ensuing fracas led to a chaotic battle with the Super Athlete at *SummerSlam* and again at *Clash of Champions*, where Rusev surrendered the title. All things considered, Roman, they probably would have preferred a blender.

WWE THE BEST OF 2016

Rusev and Roman Reigns went toe-to-toe inside the Cell in a battle for the U.S. title. Rusev was the first Superstar to win the title after it became exclusive to the *Raw* brand in 2016, but Reigns won it from him at *Clash of the Champions*.

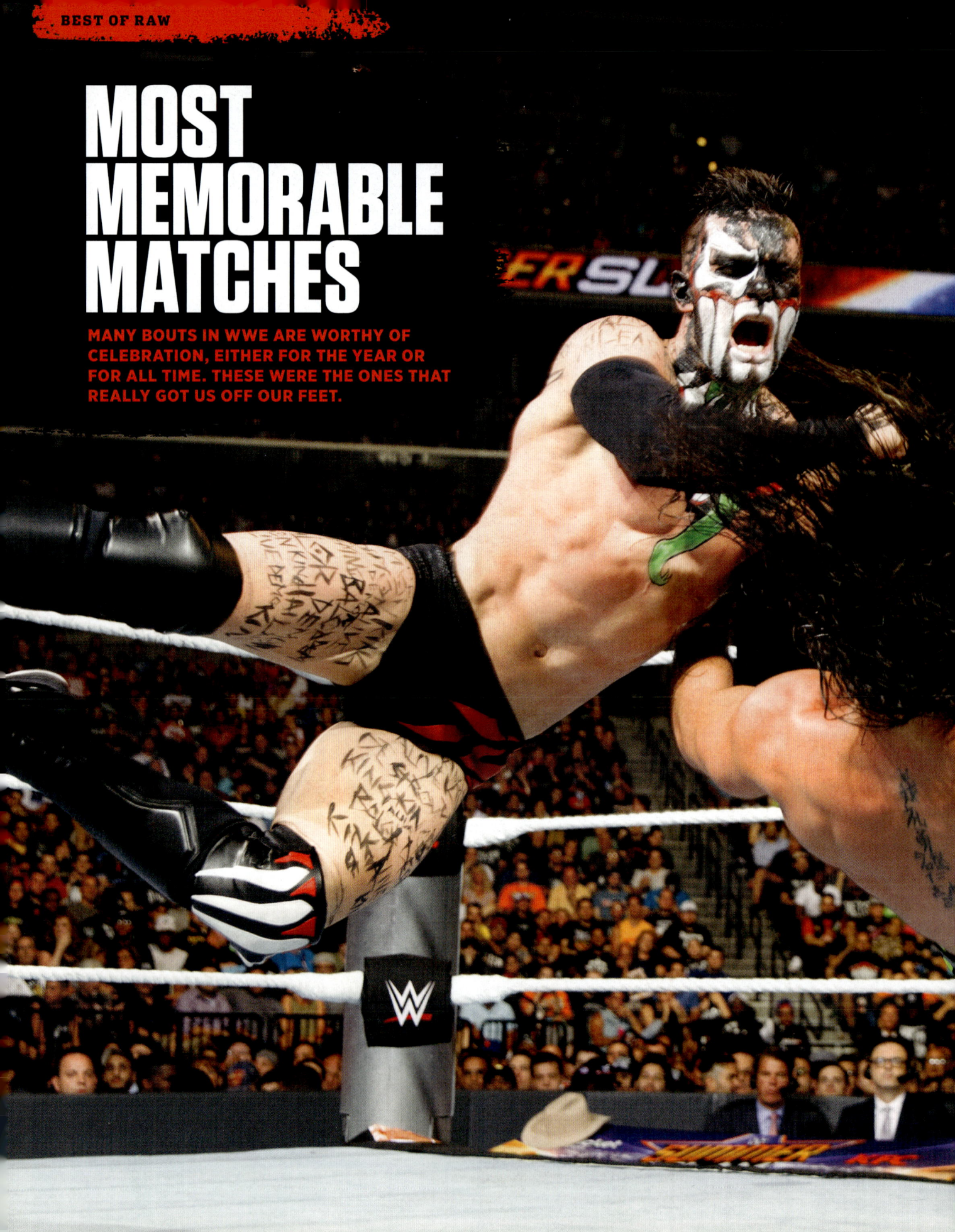

BEST OF RAW

MOST MEMORABLE MATCHES

MANY BOUTS IN WWE ARE WORTHY OF CELEBRATION, EITHER FOR THE YEAR OR FOR ALL TIME. THESE WERE THE ONES THAT REALLY GOT US OFF OUR FEET.

FINN BÁLOR VS. SETH ROLLINS
SUMMERSLAM, 8/21/16

The Demon King and the Architect faced off in a battle that, no matter what the outcome, was guaranteed to make history, considering it was for a brand-new WWE title, the Universal Championship. Forged in the aftermath of the brand split, the Universal Championship was the most coveted title on the *Raw* roster, and both Superstars were willing to fight tooth and nail to get it. With only a month on *Raw* under his belt, Bálor still entered the ring with the confidence of a vet. But Rollins used his years of experience between the ropes to his advantage. The match was a blistering back and forth that saw both Superstars put their technical skills to the test. But even Rollins's best assault couldn't hold back the fury of the Demon King. After countering the Pedigree, Bálor hit the Coupe de Grace on Rollins to win the gold and enter the WWE record books.

BEST OF RAW
MEMORABLE MATCHES

CESARO VS. SHEAMUS #7
CLASH OF CHAMPIONS, 9/25/16

The battle between Cesaro and Sheamus had the WWE Universe wondering which competitor was truly the better man. With the series tied at three apiece, Sheamus and Cesaro stepped into the ring in Indianapolis determined to settle the score. Both Superstars pulled out every move they had in their arsenal, as well as a few that weren't (Hello, 619 from Cesaro!), and it was enough to bring the bout to a no contest. Looks like we will have to wait to see who the true better man is, considering that Sheamus and Cesaro are now a team. In the end, we'll just have to consider ourselves the true winners for witnessing these incredible matchups.

Chris Jericho and Dean Ambrose's *Extreme Rules* match was billed as WWE's first-ever "Asylum Match," which featured a steel cage with weapons suspended above it.

In his match with Dolph Ziggler at *No Mercy*, The Miz added insult to injury by stealing maneuvers made famous by Daniel Bryan, including this corner dropkick.

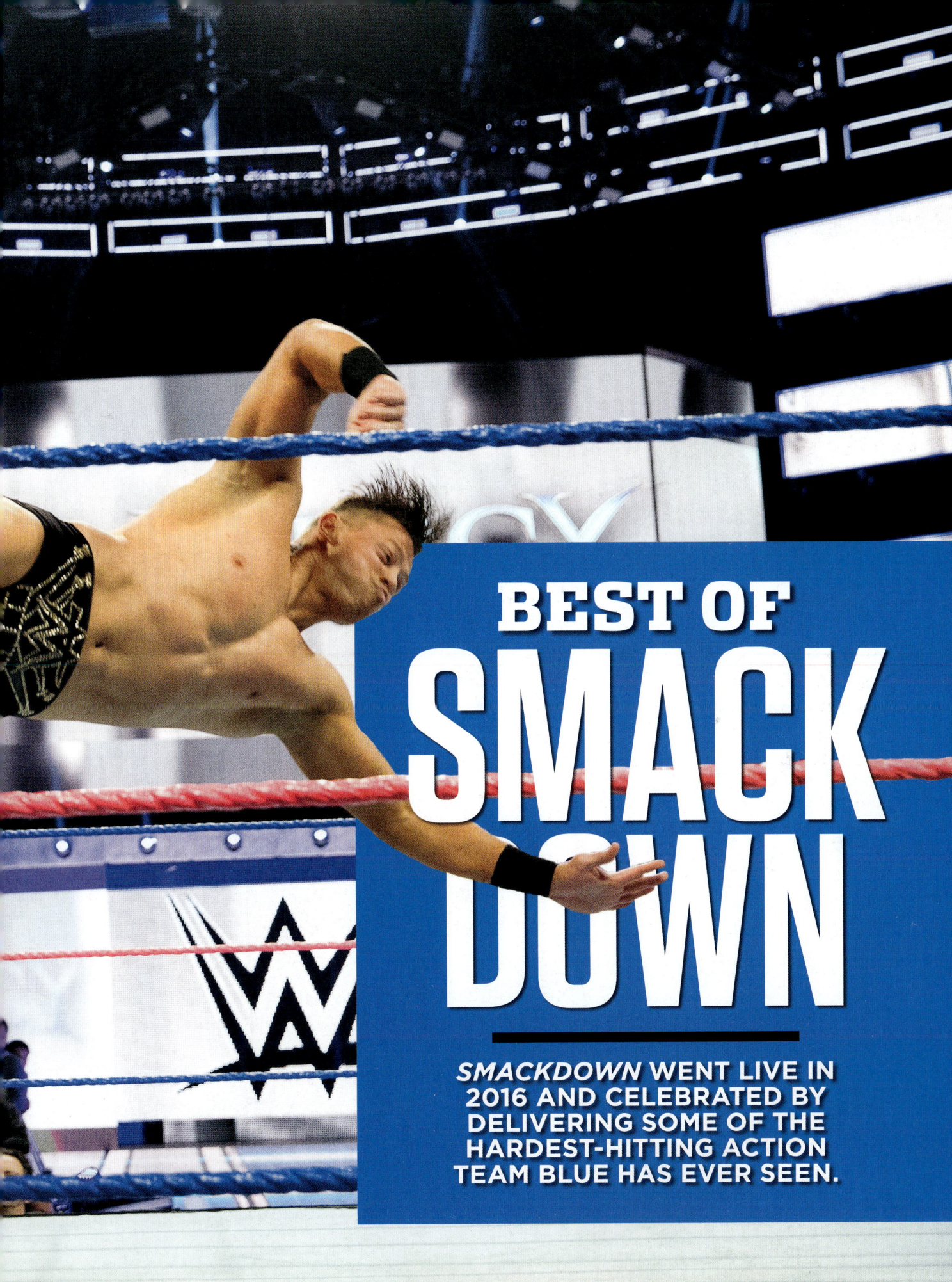

BEST OF SMACK DOWN

SMACKDOWN WENT LIVE IN 2016 AND CELEBRATED BY DELIVERING SOME OF THE HARDEST-HITTING ACTION TEAM BLUE HAS EVER SEEN.

BEST OF SMACKDOWN

STANDOUT SUPERSTARS

WHETHER IT WAS THEIR WILL TO WIN, THEIR SHEER DOMINANCE OR THEIR CONNECTION TO THE WWE UNIVERSE, THESE SUPERSTARS LEFT A LASTING IMPACT ON 2016.

RANDY ORTON
MOST LIKELY TO STRIKE OUTTA NOWHERE

When *SmackDown* recruited Randy Orton in the WWE Draft, it was a huge coup for the Blue Brand—but it came with a caveat. The third-generation Superstar reminded the WWE Universe why he's known as The Viper in October when he shockingly dropped Kane with an RKO outta nowhere, seemingly aligning himself with Orton's rival, Bray Wyatt. Could 2017 be the year Bray Wyatt becomes the most prominent voice in Orton's head?

BARON CORBIN
LEAST LIKELY TO HAVE FRIENDS IN THE LOCKER ROOM

Being the Lone Wolf of WWE has served Baron Corbin well so far, but it sure seems like the menacing Superstar goes out of his way to antagonize anyone around him. Since being drafted to *SmackDown*, Corbin has picked fights with the likes of Apollo Crews and Jack Swagger, and he's even bullied Kalisto, a man half his size. If the Lone Wolf ever finds himself at odds with a tag team, he'll likely be hard-pressed to find anyone willing to be his partner.

BEST OF SMACKDOWN

STANDOUT SUPERSTARS

ALEXA BLISS
BEST COSPLAYER

She may be devious, but Alexa Bliss at least deserves praise for her fashion sense. The "small but fierce" Superstar displayed some amazing attire in 2016 that drew inspiration from the likes of *Suicide Squad*'s Harley Quinn and horror icon Freddy Krueger. We know Bliss could easily win any costume contest, but could 2017 be the year she wins the *SmackDown* Women's Championship?

BECKY LYNCH
PUNNIEST SUPERSTAR

When she's not bringing straight fire in the ring, Becky Lynch is setting the English language ablaze with her top-notch puns. At *Backlash*, Becky showed exactly why she's called the Irish Lass Kicker when she trapped Alexa Bliss in her aptly named Disarm-Her submission maneuver to become the first *SmackDown* Women's Champion. As for 2017, it's quite likely Maiden Ireland will continue to Beck-plex her way through the competition.

BRAY WYATT
MOST LIKELY TO START A CULT

Whether he's lurking in the shadows or basking in the light of his "fireflies," Bray Wyatt is always in control. The fracturing of the Wyatt Family during the WWE Draft proved to be a non-issue for the Eater of Worlds in 2016 as he employed masterful mind games against Randy Orton on *SmackDown*. And now with longtime acolyte Luke Harper back by his side, there's no telling what destruction Wyatt is capable of in 2017.

BEST OF SMACKDOWN
TOP TAG TEAMS

AMERICAN ALPHA
MOST READY, WILLING AND GABLE

Comprised of a former Olympic wrestler and an NCAA national qualifier, American Alpha may be the purest technicians on *SmackDown*. And as former *NXT* Tag Team Champions, Jason Jordan and Chad Gable have a reputation that precedes them in WWE. Can their unmatched mat skills lead them to main roster gold in 2017?

BREEZANGO
TEAM WE NEED MORE OF

The teaming of Tyler Breeze and Fandango is a no-brainer. But where was this dapper duo for much of 2016? Probably strutting down a runway somewhere.

THE USOS
GREATEST TRANSITION

A quick defeat courtesy of American Alpha on *SmackDown* was all it took to flip a switch in The Usos. Gone are the days of vibrant face paint and call-and-response interactions with the WWE Universe—Jimmy and Jey are all business now. And if their vicious post-match attacks are any indication, they may be the team standing tallest on *SmackDown* in 2017.

SPIRIT SQUAD
MOST GROAN-WORTHY RETURN

It's probably safe to assume there wasn't a single member of the WWE Universe clamoring for the re-emergence of The Spirit Squad in 2016, but here we are. Fortunately, we only have to endure two of them instead of five this time.

HEATH SLATER & RHYNO
MOST UNLIKELY PAIRING

When Heath Slater was seemingly forgotten during the WWE Draft, it wasn't looking like 2016 would go down as his greatest year. But the One-Man Band made the most of his free agent status by recruiting Rhyno of all people for a make-or-break shot at the *SmackDown* Tag Team Championship. The duo succeeded, and Heath gained not only gold but possibly even a friend in the form of the Man Beast. But the real winners? Heath's many kids.

MOST PASSIONATE OUTPOURING

THERE CAN BE ONLY ONE FACE THAT TRULY RUNS THE PLACE

"There is no place else for me—the reason I'm here is because the words hustle, loyalty and respect are my heartbeat. I'm here out of love. What the hell are you doing here?"
—John Cena questioning AJ Styles, *SmackDown*, 08/02/16

Zack Ryder's stunning victory at *WrestleMania* marked the first time the Intercontinental Championship had ever changed hands at two consecutive 'Manias.

CARMELLA VS. NIKKI BELLA
MOST FABULOUS VS. MOST FEARLESS

When Nikki Bella made a surprise return at *SummerSlam*, the WWE Universe gave her a hero's welcome. But one person who quickly soured on the longest-reigning Divas Champion's comeback was Carmella, whom Nikki eliminated from the six-woman tag team match. In the months that followed, the Princess of Staten Island made it her mission to sneak attack The Fearless One every chance she got. The brutal beatdowns seemed to be working in Carmella's favor as she scored a handful of upset pinfalls over Nikki in tag team encounters. Finally, Nikki would get some revenge when she fought her way to a win over her formidable foe in a one-on-one match at *No Mercy*. But judging by the intensity we've already seen, this rivalry might be far from over.

BEST OF SMACKDOWN

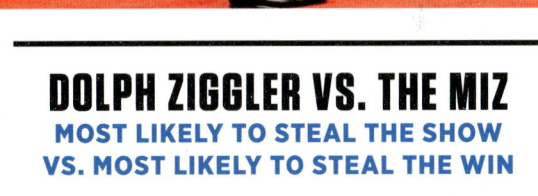

RIVETING RIVALRIES

DOLPH ZIGGLER VS. THE MIZ
MOST LIKELY TO STEAL THE SHOW VS. MOST LIKELY TO STEAL THE WIN

Despite being in their shared hometown of Cleveland, Ohio, Dolph Ziggler and The Miz were far from friendly when they came face to face on the September 27 episode of *SmackDown*. In response to a challenge for his Intercontinental Championship, the self-proclaimed A-lister belittled Ziggler's entire career, which caused The Showoff to make a daring declaration—he would put said career on the line for one more shot at the title. With the stakes higher than anyone could have predicted prior to that confrontation, the two Superstars clashed in an instant classic at *No Mercy*, pulling out every maneuver in their respective arsenals and even borrowing some from others (yes, Miz, we see your Daniel Bryan mockery). In the end, Ziggler would superkick his way to the Intercontinental Championship, but the WWE Universe were the real winners as they erupted with elation upon realizing they wouldn't have to say goodbye to The Showoff just yet. Of course, just two days later, The Miz and Maryse would rain on the parade as they donned all black and "mourned the death of the Intercontinental title." It looks like we'll be seeing more battles between these two in 2017.

WWE THE BEST OF 2016   41

BEST OF SMACKDOWN

MEMORABLE MATCHES

ALEXA BLISS VS. NAOMI VS. NIKKI BELLA VS. BECKY LYNCH VS. CARMELLA VS. NATALYA
SMACKDOWN WOMEN'S CHAMPIONSHIP
BACKLASH, 09/11/16

The first *SmackDown*-exclusive pay-per-view event of 2016 kicked off in thrilling fashion as six of the Blue Brand's female Superstars competed for the brand new Women's Championship. Contested under elimination rules, the match inspired a nearly chaotic pace that saw the likes of a picturesque sunset flip powerbomb by Alexa Bliss, a jaw-jacking superkick by Carmella and a diving crossbody to the outside of the ring by Naomi. But the most effective maneuver of the match proved to be Becky Lynch's Disarm-Her, which forced Alexa Bliss to tap out, giving The Irish Lass Kicker the win and the championship. Perhaps even more gratifying was Becky's emotional post-match victory speech, during which the WWE Universe showered her with chants of "YOU DESERVE IT" as she proudly declared herself "Becky Balboa."

AJ STYLES VS. DEAN AMBROSE VS. JOHN CENA
WWE WORLD CHAMPIONSHIP
NO MERCY, 10/09/16

Heading into *No Mercy*, tensions between the WWE World Champion AJ Styles, Dean Ambrose and John Cena were at a fever pitch. The Phenomenal One and The Cenation Leader had already proven their disdain for each other over the summer, but the beef between Cena and Ambrose was a newer development—and one Styles was sure to capitalize on. When the three finally collided at *No Mercy*, the tumultuous tension manifested in a match for the ages that saw amazing maneuver after amazing maneuver and near fall after near fall. In the end, the sly Styles, perhaps out of desperation to keep his title, took advantage of the no-disqualification caveat of triple threat rules to blast Cena with a chair and score the 1-2-3.

WWE THE BEST OF 2016   51

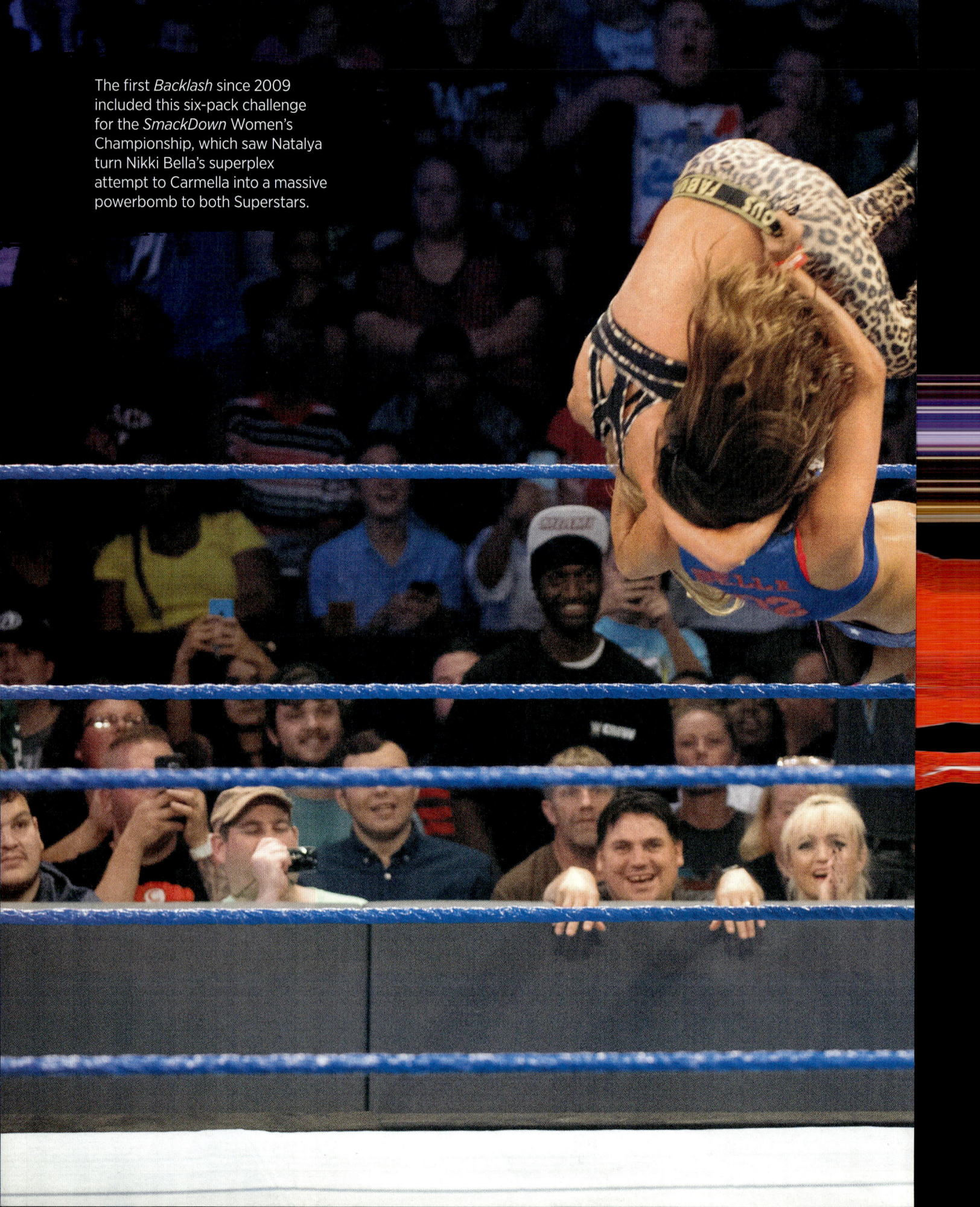

The first *Backlash* since 2009 included this six-pack challenge for the *SmackDown* Women's Championship, which saw Natalya turn Nikki Bella's superplex attempt to Carmella into a massive powerbomb to both Superstars.

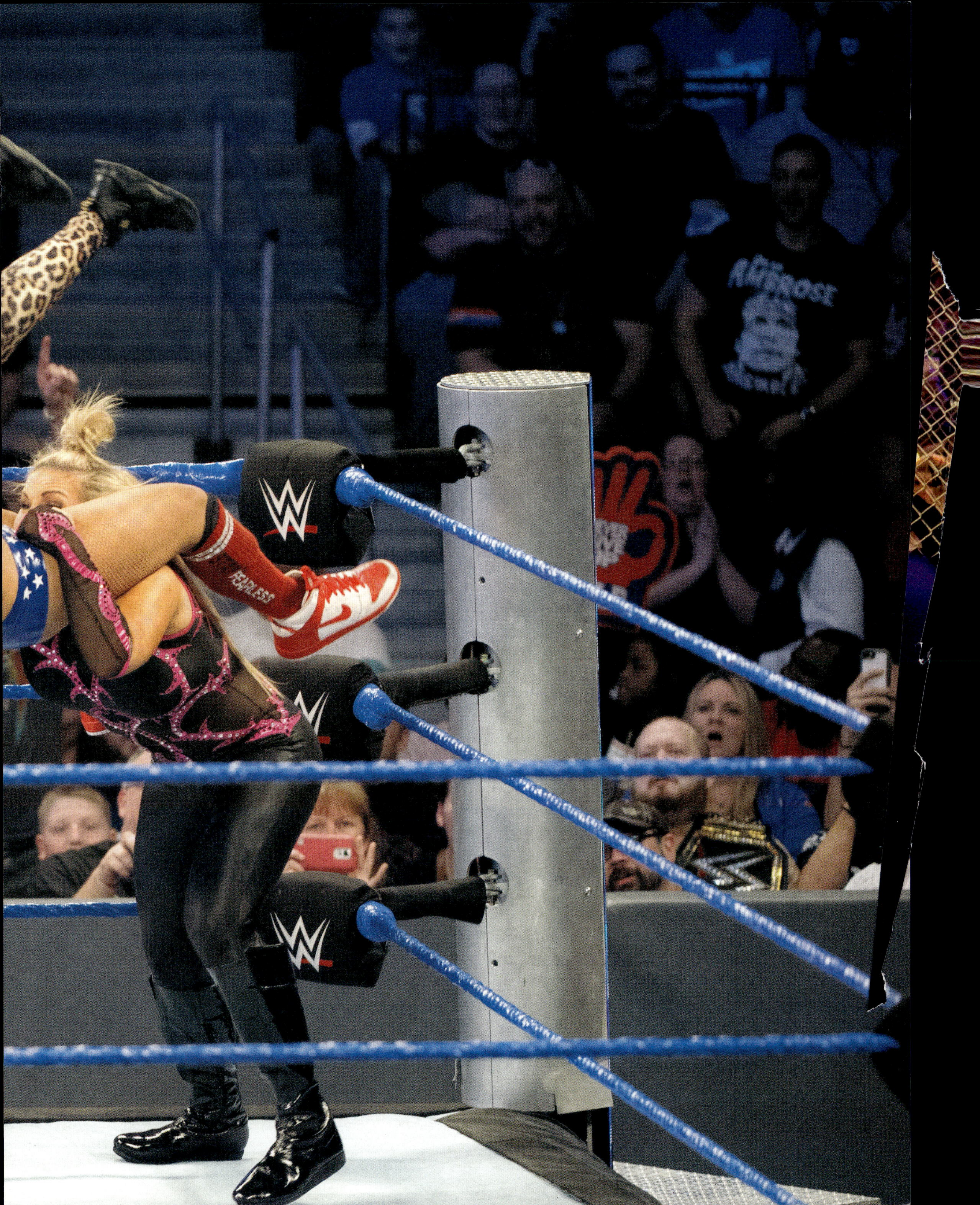
AMBROSE
FEARLESS

At *NXT: TakeOver: Brooklyn II*, Ember Moon makes a memorable debut, facing Billie Kay. Moon displayed equal parts brutality and athleticism, walking out a winner.

BEST OF NXT

NXT EXPLODED IN 2016, SHOWCASING HIGH-FLYING AND GROUND-POUNDING ACTION THAT WILL SHAPE THE FUTURE OF WWE.

BEST OF NXT

SUPERSTARS

MEET THE FAST-RISING SUPERSTARS WHO SHOOK UP THE SYSTEM IN 2016 AND ARE POISED TO ROCK THE WWE UNIVERSE IN 2017.

56 WWE THE BEST OF 2016

EMBER MOON
MOST MYSTERIOUS

Exotic and alluring, Ember Moon debuted at *NXT TakeOver: Brooklyn II* and immediately drew the attention of the WWE Universe. Her athleticism and in-ring ability has already shown that, despite her enigmatic demeanor, the fact that Ember Moon belongs in WWE is no mystery at all.

"THE GREATEST MAN WHO EVER LIVED" AUSTIN ARIES
MOST HYPERBOLIC NICKNAME

As The Miz once said, "Really?" By calling himself by this rather immodest moniker, Aries is placing himself above such WWE legends as The Rock, Stone Cold and Triple H. Not to mention…well, every other man who has trod the earth. That's not to say he doesn't approach greatness in the ring. Aries definitely has skill, and, as his dominant in-ring performances have shown, he'll definitely make an impact when he hits the main roster. Greatest Man Who Ever Lived? Debatable. But Greatest Superstar? It could happen.

NO WAY JOSE
BEST PARTY STARTER

With his fast-footed dance moves and love of a good time, No Way Jose seems like he'd be as much fun to hang out with as he is to watch in the ring. As evidenced by his Conga Line entrance at *NXT Takeover: Brooklyn II*, Jose knows how to get the party started. And, like any good Superstar, when the bell rings, he knows when it's time for business.

THE REVIVAL
TAG TEAM OF THE YEAR

Combining Dash Wilder's mountain-bred battling style and Scott Dawson's streetwise fighting smarts, The Revival is a team that has ignited *NXT*'s tag scene over the last year. After an impressive showing at the 2015 Dusty Rhodes Tag Team Classic, they continued working their way through other teams on the roster, eventually winning the tag titles by defeating The Vaudevillains in November of that year (although they lost them to American Alpha in the spring). In 2016, they continued their ascent, eventually winning back the gold from American Alpha and becoming the first two-time *NXT* tag champs. What's next? Total domination.

BEST OF NXT

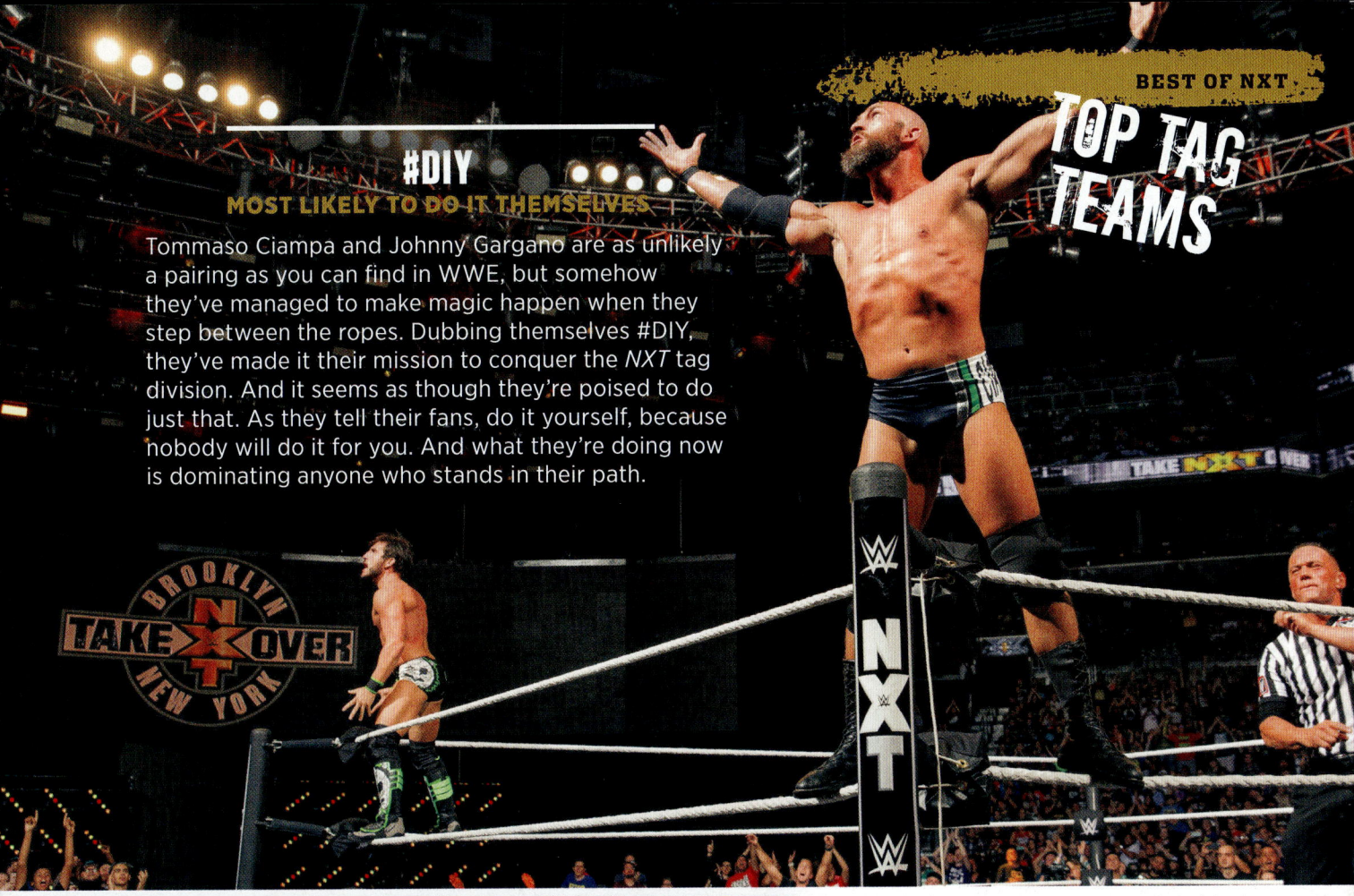

TOP TAG TEAMS

#DIY
MOST LIKELY TO DO IT THEMSELVES

Tommaso Ciampa and Johnny Gargano are as unlikely a pairing as you can find in WWE, but somehow they've managed to make magic happen when they step between the ropes. Dubbing themselves #DIY, they've made it their mission to conquer the *NXT* tag division. And it seems as though they're poised to do just that. As they tell their fans, do it yourself, because nobody will do it for you. And what they're doing now is dominating anyone who stands in their path.

GLORIOUS 10
BEST TEAM THAT NEVER WAS

Bobby Roode and Tye Dillinger could have been glorious together, possibly even perfect. When the Perfect 10 was approached by Roode to form a partnership, the offer seemed too good to pass up and too good to be true. Unfortunately dreams were dashed when, during a beatdown from SAnitY, Dillinger put out his hand to his new partner, hoping for some backup. Roode, however, had other ideas, and walked out, ending the partnership before it even had a chance to begin. Let's hope their rivalry is as awesome as their partnership could have been.

WWE THE BEST OF 2016   59

"YOU...TALK... TOO MUCH!"

—ASUKA, LAYING IT OUT PLAIN AND SIMPLE FOR NIA JAX, *NXT*, 6/1/16

BEST OF NXT

MIC DROPS

62 WWE THE BEST OF 2016

BEST OF NXT

RIVETING RIVALRIES

SHINSUKE NAKAMURA VS. SAMOA JOE
CHAMPIONSHIP QUEST TURNED ALL-OUT WAR

Witnessing the King of Strong Style and the Samoan Submission Specialist colliding in combat was a dream come true for the WWE Universe. Samoa Joe was already ruling the ring as *NXT* champion when GM William Regal named Nakamura next up to challenge for the title. Joe was outraged, believing that Nakamura didn't have what it took to hold the *NXT* title. Nevertheless, the die had been cast, and Joe was told he would face Nakamura or relinquish the gold. With no other choice, the two went head to head the night before *SummerSlam* at *NXT TakeOver: Brooklyn II*. The two Superstars applied their hard-hitting smash mouth offenses to the bout, with each one kicking out of the other's finisher. But it was Nakamura who managed to win it all, taking Joe out with a Kinshasa to take home the title. Nakamura's victory made him the first Japanese Superstar ever to hold a world title.

The Revival managed to retain the tag titles at *NXT Takeover: Brooklyn II*, defeating Johnny Gargano and Tommaso Ciampa. The Revival is the first *NXT* team to hold the titles more than once.

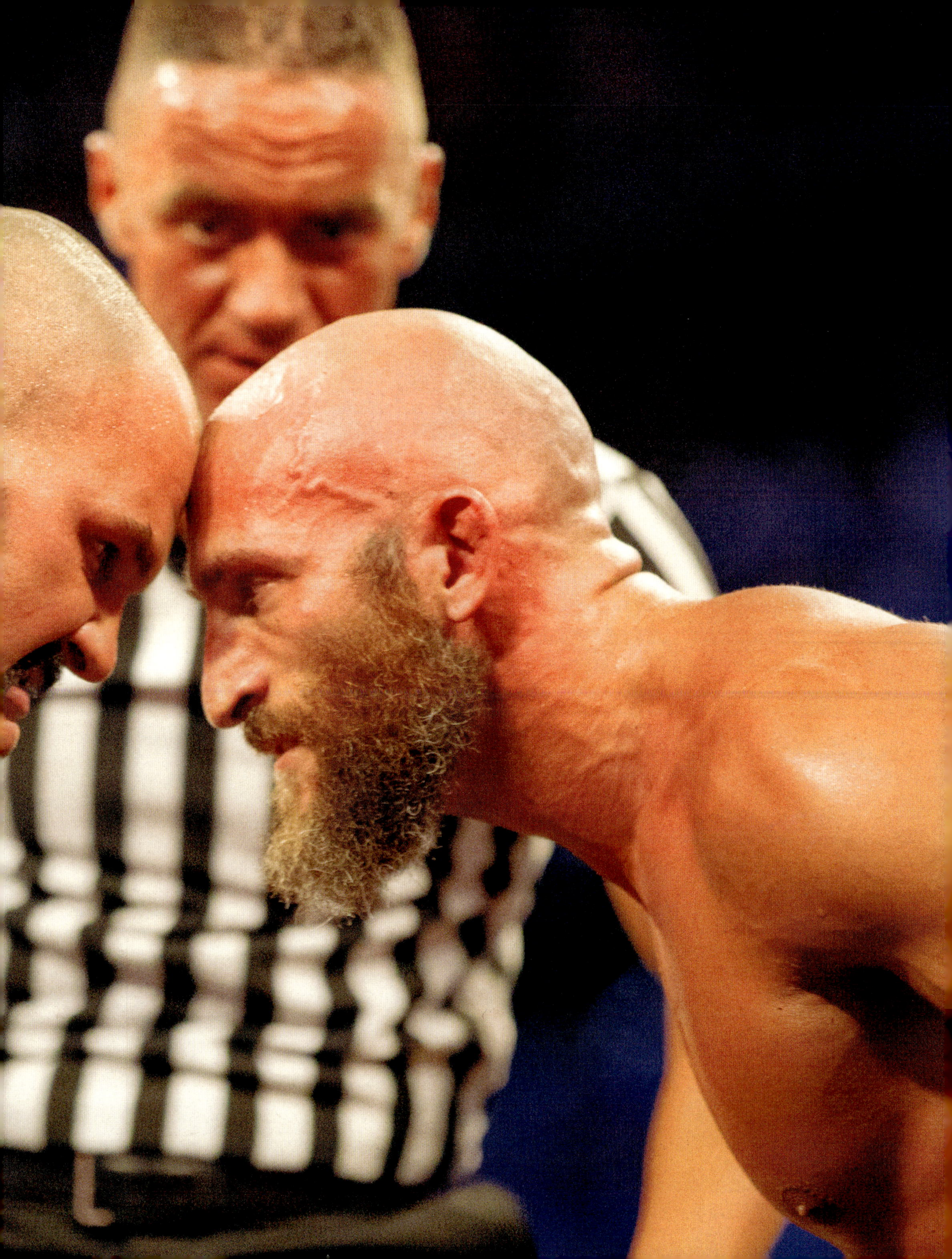

BEST OF NXT

MEMORABLE MATCHES

SAMI ZAYN VS. SHINSUKE NAKAMURA
NXT TAKEOVER: DALLAS, 04/01/16

As debuts go, it doesn't get much better than Shinsuke Nakamura's explosive bow at the Dallas *TakeOver*. Expectations were high for the King of Strong Style, and he did not disappoint. Both Nakamura and Zayn matched high-flying acrobatics with a sustained ground attack, delivering a match that thrilled in and above the ring. The match had Triple H himself riveted backstage! Ultimately, it was Nakamura who picked up the win, laying out Zayn with a devastating Kinshasa. Gracious in defeat, Zayn embraced his competitor in a show of respect.

BEST OF NXT

MEMORABLE MATCHES

BAYLEY VS. ASUKA
NXT TAKEOVER: BROOKLYN II, 08/20/16

Some might have thought the diminutive, bubbly Bayley might have been outmatched by the brutish, almost bullyish tactics of Asuka. But when the bell rang at the second *Brooklyn TakeOver*, Bayley showed that she wasn't there to give out hugs. What followed was an all-out slugfest, with both women giving as good as they got. After taking some abuse from the Empress of Tomorrow, Bayley came into Brooklyn not about to take another second, even going so far as to dare Asuka to hit her in the face. Asuka gladly obliged, but found Bayley to be a more daunting foe than she perhaps originally imagined. The Hugster even managed to get out of the Asuka Lock twice! Sadly for Bayley, the Empress connected with two unforgiving headshots, leaving her opponent out cold. A bad day for Bayley, but a great night for the WWE Universe.

WWE THE BEST OF 2016 69

No Way Jose has always prided himself on being able to start a party, and he did so in grand style at *NXT: TakeOver Brooklyn II*, starting a conga line that snaked its way through the Barclays Center.

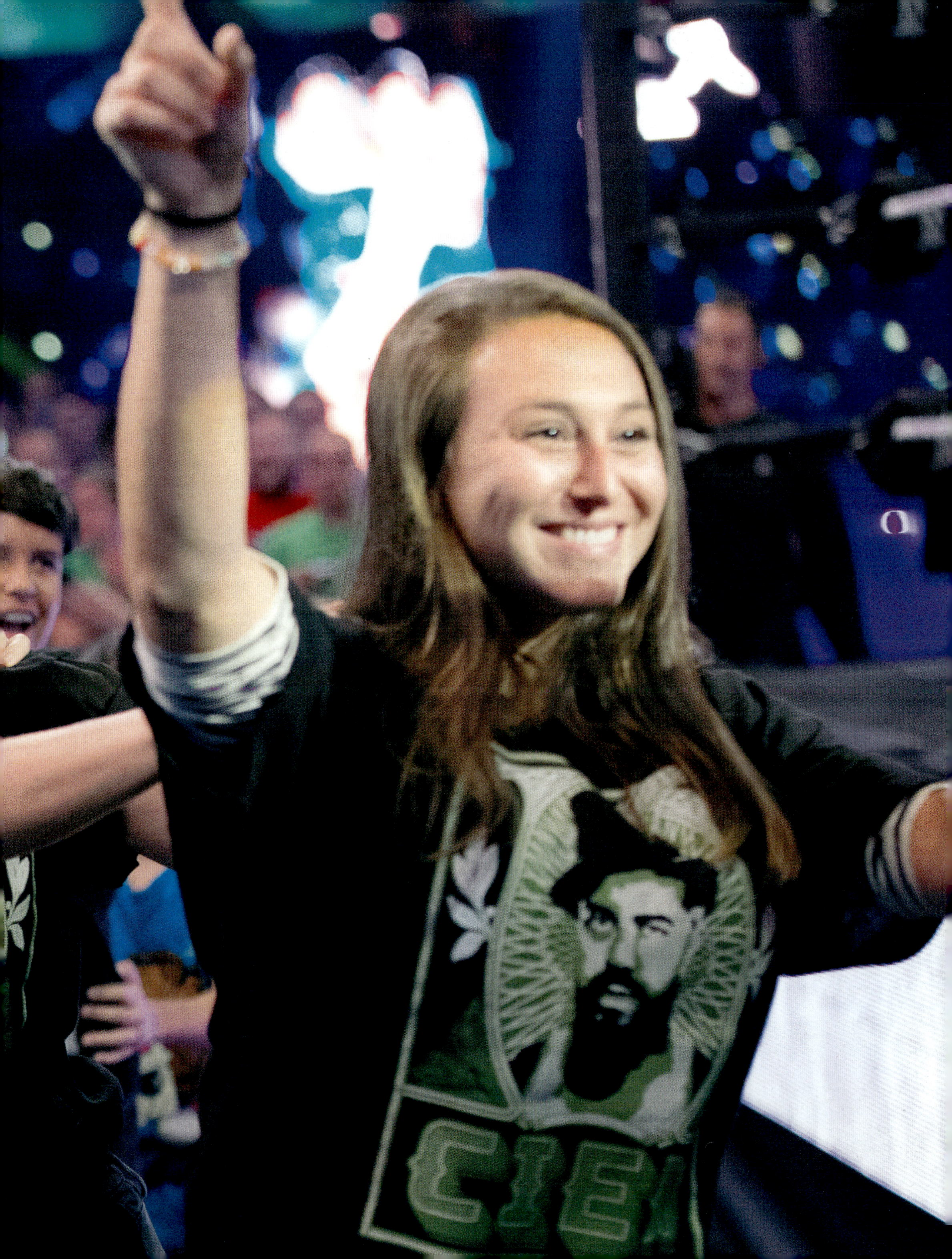

On the August 29 edition of *Raw*, Triple H gave Kevin Owens an assist to win the vacant Universal Championship. Owens is one of only three Superstars to hold both an NXT and WWE world title.

BEST OF THE BEST

FROM BRUTAL BETRAYALS TO CEILING-SHATTERING WOMEN, 2016 WAS A YEAR THAT TOOK WWE TO A WHOLE NEW LEVEL. HERE ARE THE AWARD-WINNING MOMENTS THAT MADE THE GRADE THIS YEAR.

BEST DRESSED
ENZO AMORE

While he might not dress in silk shirts like The Rock or sport a killer Armani suit like Triple H, Enzo manages to take an ensemble that's as flashy as it is ostentatious and somehow make it look ready for a runway in Milan. From leather jackets to a different pair of kicks every week, Enzo's wardrobe is almost a character in itself. Who knows? Maybe 2017 will be the year where he adds some extra bling to go with his getups. The kind that's shaped like a championship, maybe?

BEST OF THE BEST

OUTBURST OF THE YEAR

THE MIZ ON TALKING SMACK, 8/23/16

After Daniel Bryan took a shot at Miz's wrestling style, The Miz exploded on the *SmackDown* GM, getting directly in his face and calling him a coward. "Why don't you quit and go to the bingo halls with your indie friends?" he spat. After Bryan threw up his hands and walked away, The Miz looked right into the camera and barked "This is day 141 of the never-ending Intercontinental Championship world tour, and I promise you, I swear to you, it will be the most relevant title on *SmackDown Live*!" It was a fiery, intense tirade that recalled the glory days of Piper or Flair. We always knew Miz had the gift of gab, but, until that night, we never knew how well he could turn words into weapons.

BEST OF THE BEST

TAG TEAM OF THE YEAR

THE NEW DAY

This was the year The New Day went from punchlines to players, and now that they've arrived, there's no stopping them. From their dominant in-ring performance, to two tag titles, to scads and scads of fast-selling merch (Booty-O's, anyone?), The New Day is more than a tag team at this point. They're a bona fide franchise.

WWE THE BEST OF 2016   77

BIG DEBUT

FINN BÁLOR

Already a sensation in *NXT*, the Demon King exploded onto the main roster in the summer of 2016 and quickly made his presence known. After being drafted to *Raw*, Bálor plowed his way through Rusev, Cesaro and Kevin Owens in a fatal-four-way match and then took down Roman Reigns in the main event for a shot at the Universal Title at *SummerSlam*. All in one night. In the ring in Brooklyn, Bálor proved his double victories from the month before were no fluke, defeating Seth Rollins and becoming WWE's first-ever Universal champ. Unfortunately a shoulder injury took him out of action the very next night. But, come 2017, we have no doubt that Bálor's incredible debut will prove to have been only the beginning.

BEST OF THE BEST

COMBACK OF THE YEAR

GOLDBERG

They always say "Never say never" in WWE. But, in the case of Goldberg, we all felt pretty confident in saying that we'd never again see him in a WWE ring. After an ignominious exit at *WrestleMania XX*, it seemed Goldberg was done with the business once and for all. Years of speculation and anticipation produced nothing substantial, and the WWE Universe was prepared to accept that they'd seen the last of the explosive Superstar and one of the most iconic competitors produced by the Monday Night War. Then, on the October 25 episode of *Raw*, the unthinkable happened. Goldberg returned to WWE after a 12-year absence, challenging Brock Lesnar to a match at *Survivor Series*. But just when we thought the return itself was the shocking part, Goldberg slayed The Beast in a display of complete dominance, scoring the 1-2-3 after just two spears and a Jackhammer. So, in 2017, who's next?

HONORABLE MENTION
SHANE McMAHON

Shane's return on the February 22 edition of *Raw* was the best post-holiday gift the WWE Universe could have asked for. Brash, entertaining and completely fearless to the point of brazenness in the ring, Shane was always a performer who, whether on the mic or leaping from the Titantron, was guaranteed to deliver. Since his return, delivered he has, from his heartstopping Hell in a Cell match against Undertaker at *WrestleMania* to his stint as the Commissioner of *SmackDown*, which even saw him step onto the front lines for his team at *Survivor Series*. Welcome back, Shane-O-Mac!

80 WWE THE BEST OF 2016

BEST OF THE BEST

RIVALRY OF THE YEAR
SASHA BANKS VS. CHARLOTTE FLAIR

In 2016, the glass ceiling that once hovered over WWE was completely shattered—and we're still picking the shards out of our popcorn. Sasha Banks and Charlotte Flair took Women's Competition not just to a new level, but an entirely new plane of existence. Their rivalry had already offered unforgettable matchups that showcased their formidable in-ring ability, but the two women completely changed the game when they competed in the first-ever Women's Hell in a Cell match at the *Hell in a Cell* network event in October. The bout, which saw Flair claim victory, set an entirely new standard in WWE—not just for females, but for all Superstars.

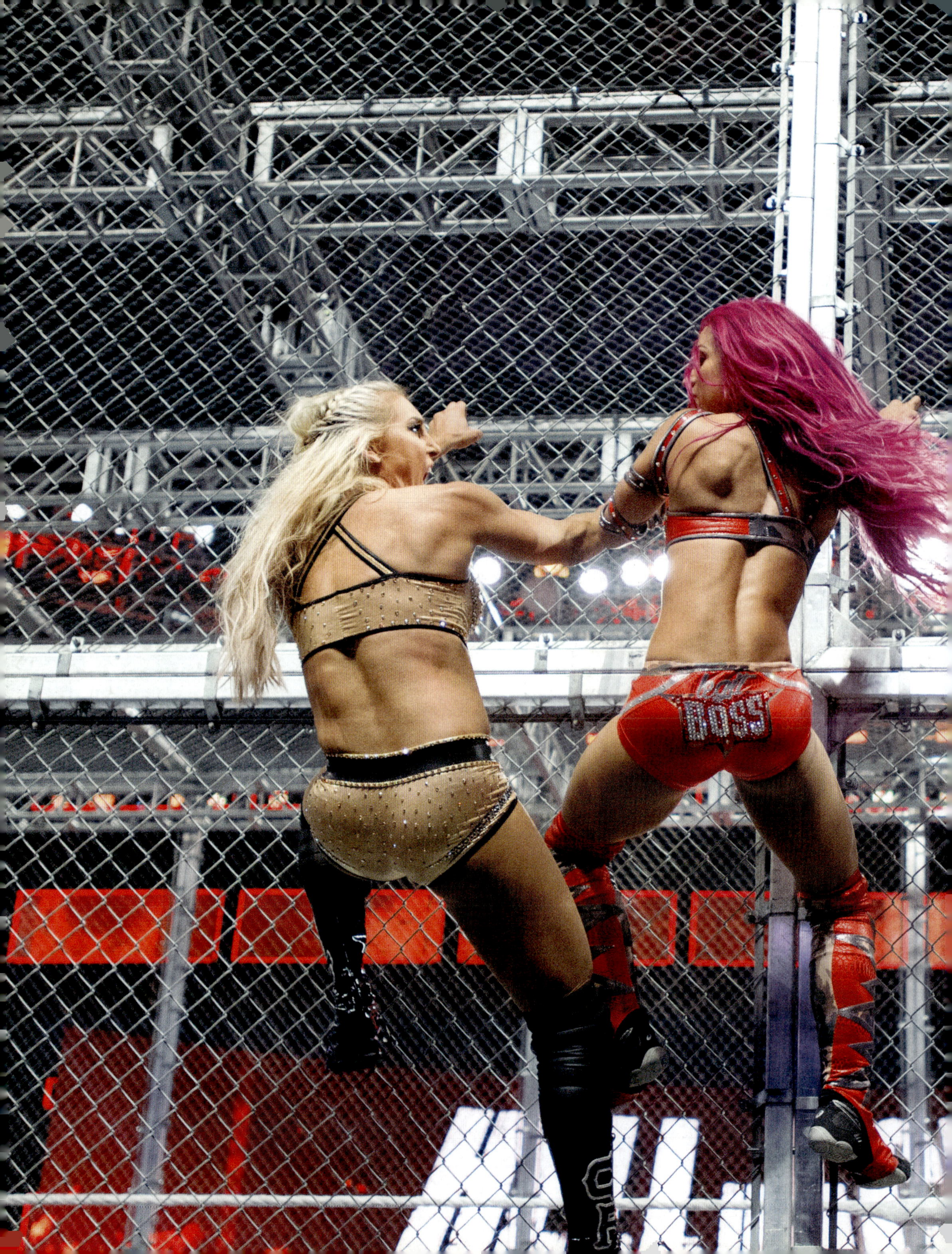
BOSS

> At *Hell in a Cell*, Charlotte and Sasha destroyed expectations. Not only are they the first women ever to compete in the Cell, they're also the first women ever to main event a WWE PPV!

84 WWE THE BEST OF 2016

BEST OF THE BEST

BIGGEST SHOCKER
TRIPLE H TAKES KEVIN OWENS TO THE TOP

With the vacating of the Universal Championship, a fatal four-way for the title was held the week after *SummerSlam*. Kevin Owens, Big Cass, Seth Rollins and Roman Reigns squared off to vie for the gold, with the winner taking home *Raw*'s most coveted prize. Reigns proved to be a dominant player in the match, to the point that most WWE Universe members believed he was about to win it all. That's when, upending everyone's expectations, Triple H made his return to *Raw*. With Reigns, Rollins and Owens the only players left, The Game served Reigns with a Pedigree, taking him out of the mix. Most assumed the move was designed to set Rollins up for the win. However, it seemed he had other plans. Triple H shocked the world when he turned on Rollins, delivering another Pedigree and letting Owens make the pinfall. The move showed the WWE Universe one thing: No one is safe.

BEST OF THE BEST

MATCH OF THE YEAR

AJ STYLES VS. JOHN CENA AT *SUMMERSLAM*

Styles and Cena met up in a match that wasn't about titles or accolades. The only thing on the line was pride. After months of acrimony, everything collided in the ring at the Barclay's Center. This was a match the WWE had been waiting for, and neither competitor let them down. Each one pounded the other with their finishers multiple times, but neither could seal the deal. Back and forth they went. An Attitude Adjustment became a suplex, a Phenomenal Forearm became an STF. This was one match where no one could guess the winner and everything was up for grabs. Finally, another Attitude Adjustment reversal set Styles up to deliver a Phenomenal Forearm to beat Cena 1-2-3. It was an unbelievable upset and a true signal for the dawning of a new era in WWE.

WWE THE BEST OF 2016 **87**

BEST OF THE BEST

88 WWE THE BEST OF 2016

JERK OF THE YEAR

KEVIN OWENS

We almost hate to call him a jerk, because the truth is, we kind of have to respect how good he is at being one. From his penchant for betrayal, to his unholy alliances with the likes of Triple H and Chris Jericho, Owens has made being underhanded, untrustworthy and unlikeable into an art form. And that's to say nothing about his in-ring ability. Owens moves with the raw fury of a charging bull, not caring who he mows down or the kind of devastation he leaves in his wake. Bottom line, in the ring and out of it, Owens is only looking out for himself. Of course, given his run as WWE Universal Champion, one could argue that Owens's vile ways have brought him far. But we'd rather look ahead to who is going to bring him down.

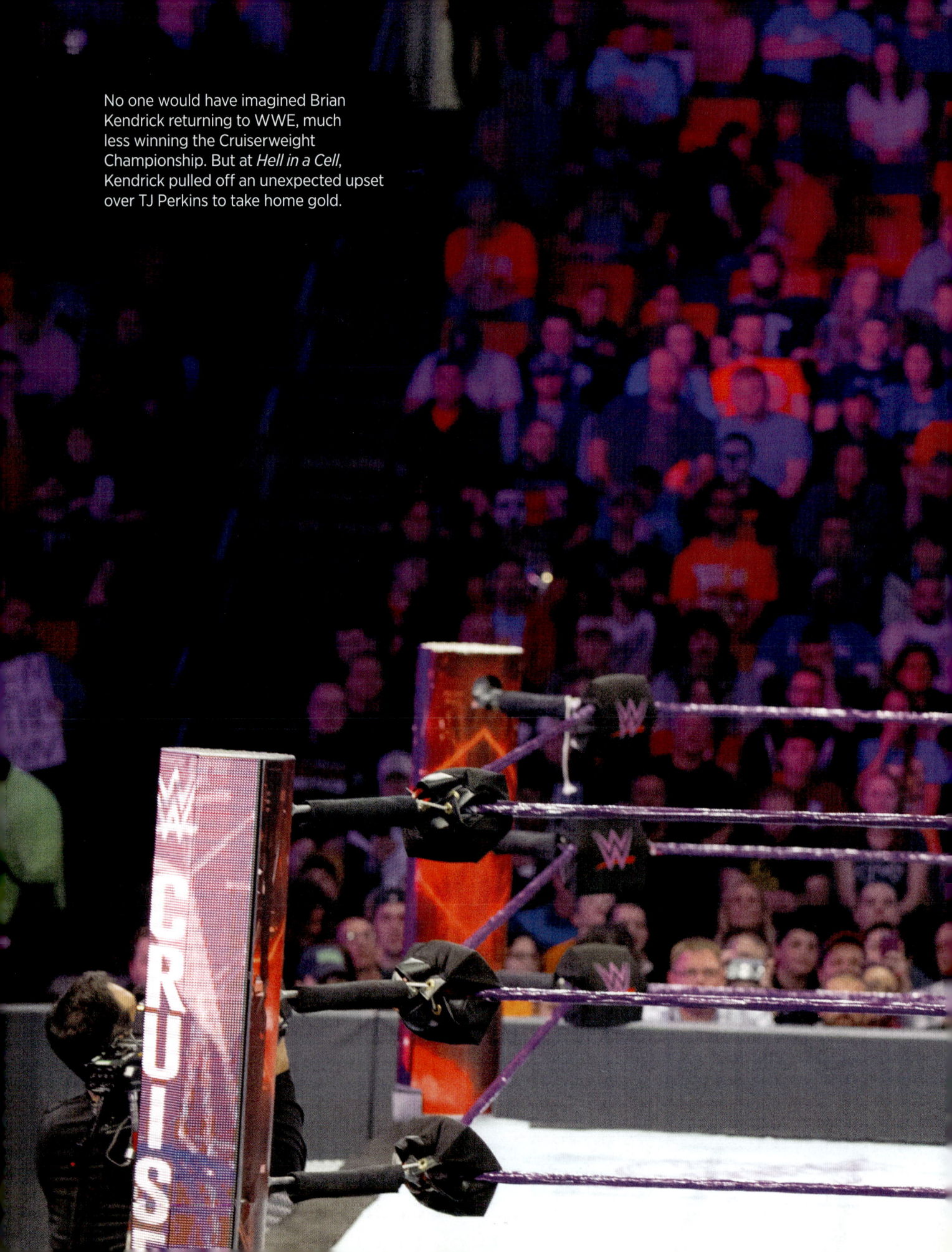

No one would have imagined Brian Kendrick returning to WWE, much less winning the Cruiserweight Championship. But at *Hell in a Cell*, Kendrick pulled off an unexpected upset over TJ Perkins to take home gold.

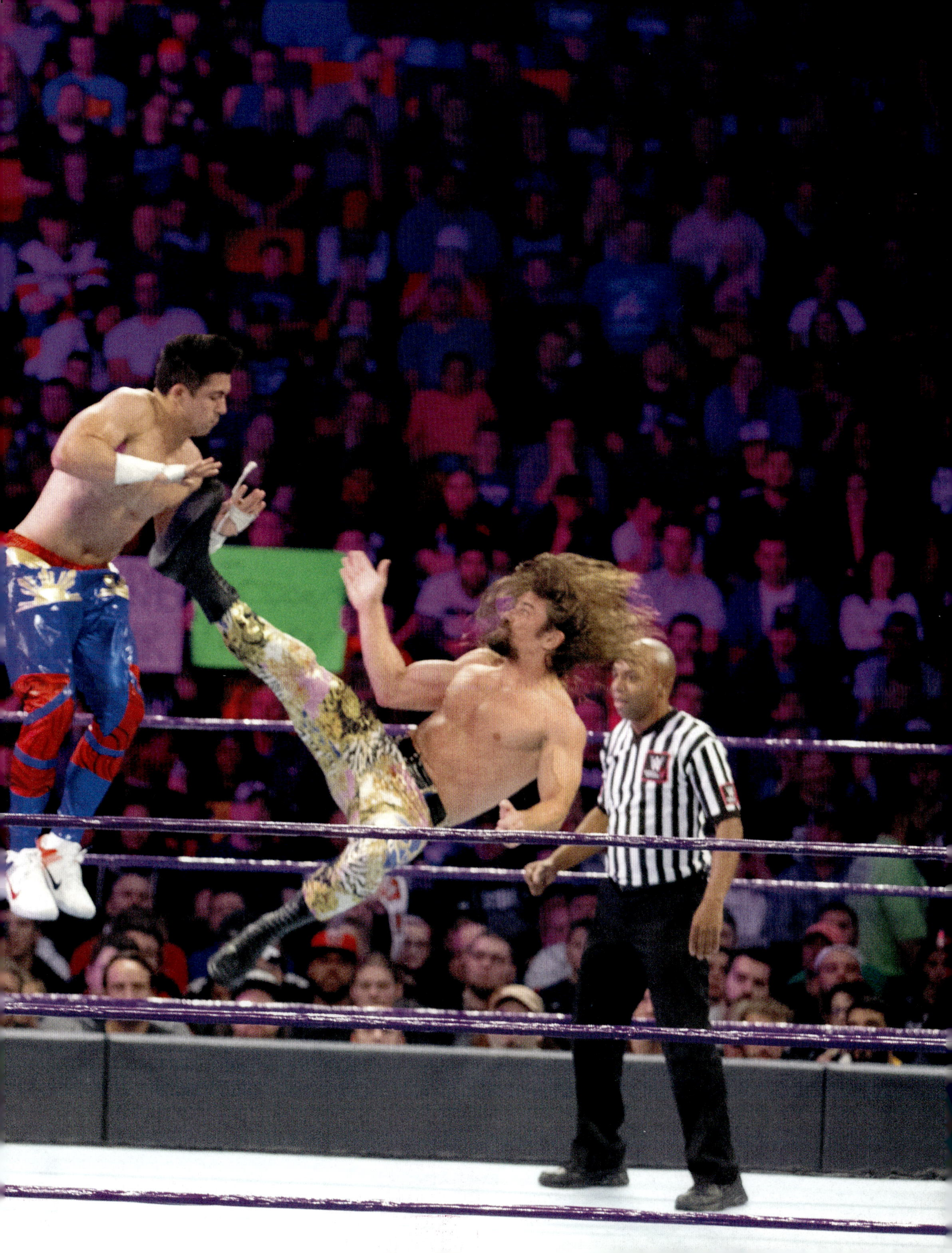

BEST OF THE BEST

SUPERSTAR OF THE YEAR

AJ STYLES

When AJ Styles made his debut at the 2016 *Royal Rumble*, the WWE Universe expected great things, and Styles, a longtime ring vet with experience that covers the globe, did not disappoint. After an incredible rivalry with John Cena, Styles leapt into the title picture in the fall, defeating Dean Ambrose at *Backlash* to win his first WWE Championship. The victory was a significant one, as it represented the arrival of a Superstar who had been championed by the WWE Universe long before the powers that be decided to give him a shot. Since then, he's continued riding high with multiple title defenses and seen his star continue to rise in WWE. Many times, a fan-favorite Superstar makes an explosive debut then fizzles out. But a rare few just fly higher and higher until you realize it's hard to imagine WWE without them. Have a look at AJ Styles and tell us which one you think he is.

A Topix Media Lab Publication
For inquiries, call 646-476-8860

TOPIX MEDIA LAB

CEO Tony Romando

Vice President of Brand Marketing Joy Bomba
Director of Finance Vandana Patel
Director of Sales and New Markets Tom Mifsud
Manufacturing Director Nancy Puskuldjian
Financial Analyst Matthew Quinn
Brand Marketing Assistant Taylor Hamilton

Editor-in-Chief Jeff Ashworth
Creative Director Steven Charny
Photo Director Dave Weiss
Managing Editor Courtney Kerrigan
Senior Editors Tim Baker, James Ellis

Issue Editor Jeremy Brown
Issue Photo Editor Meg Reinhardt
Art Director Susan Dazzo
Assistant Managing Editor Holland Baker
Senior Designer Michelle Lock
Designer Danielle Santucci
Assistant Photo Editor Catherine Armanasco
Photo Assistant Julia Pressman
Assistant Editors Trevor Courneen, Alicia Kort, Kaytie Norman
Editorial Assistant Isabella Torchia

Co-Founders Bob Lee, Tony Romando

WWE COLLECTOR'S EDITION

Global Publishing Manager Steve Pantaleo
Vice President of Licensing, North America Jess Richardson

Topix Media Lab Special #13, 2017. WWE Collector's Edition published by Topix Media Lab, 14 Wall Street, Suite 4B, New York, NY 10005. All rights reserved. No material in this issue may be reprinted without the written permission of the publisher. Entire contents copyright © 2017. Certain photographs used in this publication are used by license or permission from the owner thereof, or are otherwise publicly available. Topix Media Lab is not affiliated with, nor sponsored or endorsed by, any of the persons, entities, product names, logos, brands or other trademarks featured or referred to in any of its publications. PRINTED IN THE USA.

©2017 World Wrestling Entertainment, Inc., 1241 East Main Street, Stamford, Connecticut, USA 06902. All Rights Reserved. Published and distributed by Topix Media Lab LLC, with permission of World Wrestling Entertainment, Inc. Reproduction in whole or in part in any language without permission is prohibited.

Cover: Photography by Craig Ambrosio, Scott Brinegar, Rich Freeda, Mike Marques;
Digital Imaging by Eric Heintz
Back Cover: Photography by Eric Johnson
Goldberg Poster: Digital Imaging by Michelle Lock
Shane McMahon Poster: Photography by John Giamundo

Craig Ambrosio: 31, 57, 58, 59, 62, 76; Scott Brinegar: 33, 35, 74; Rich Freeda: 14, 16, 56, 57, 59, 64, 68, 69, 70, 79, 81; John Giamundo: 20, 28, 51, 72, 79, 80, 81, 84; David Gunn: 13, 33, 40, 52, 54, 95; Melissa Halladay: 96; Eric Johnson: 2, 4, 6, 10, 11, 13, 22, 23, 24, 30, 34, 60, 86, 90, 93, 98; Mike Marques: 15, 26, 42, 66, 67, 82; Heather McLaughlin: 12, 15, 19, 25, 32, 35, 36, 41; Craig Melvin: 8, 17, 18, 34, 38, 78, 88, 92; Shutterstock

Brock Lesnar had some explosive matches in 2016, but none more anticipated than his bout against Goldberg at *Survivor Series*, their first since *WrestleMania XX* in 2004.

Dean Ambrose's unexpected cash-in at *Money in the Bank* netted him the WWE Championship and ended Seth Rollins's reign at just two minutes.

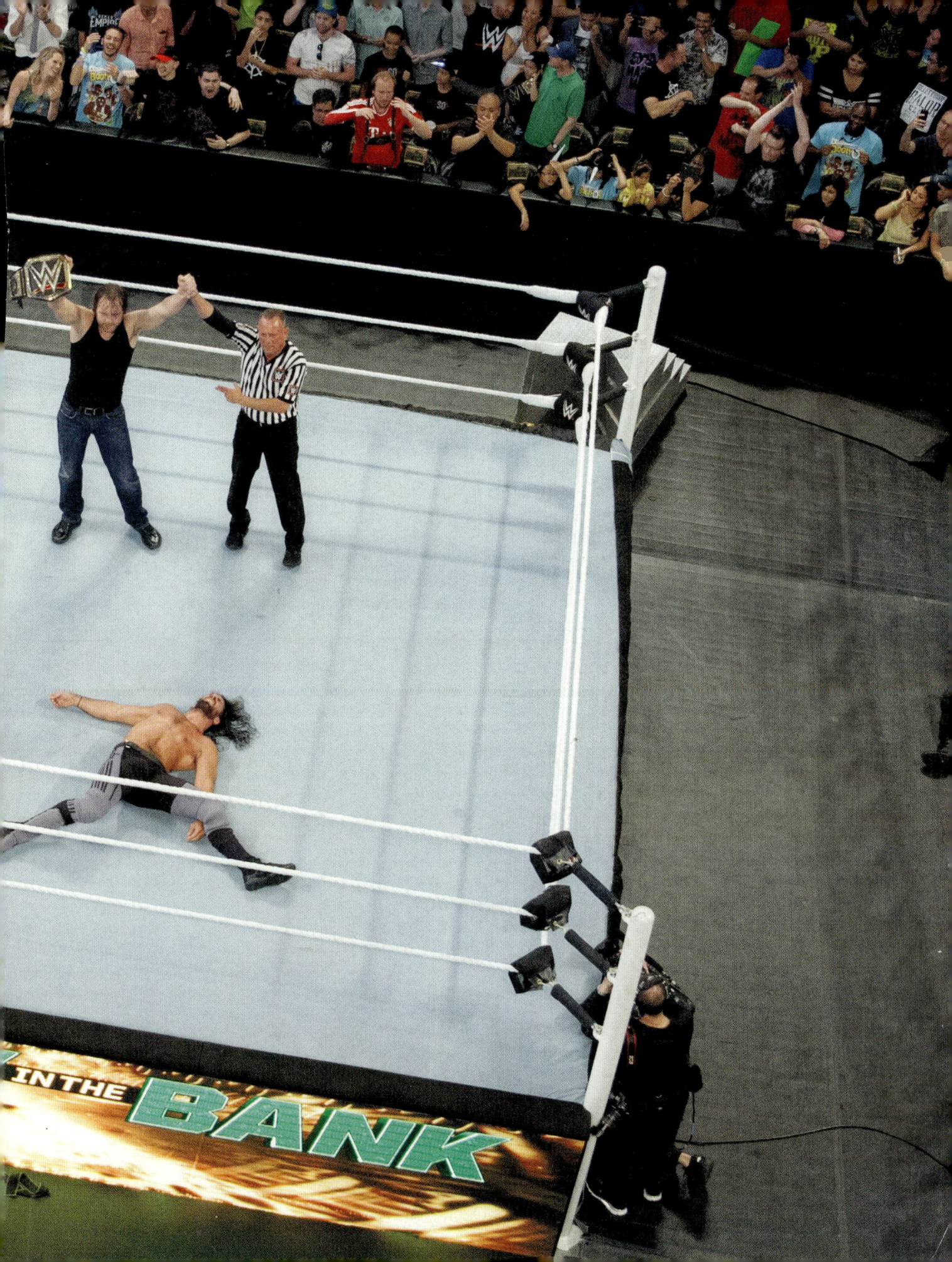

SummerSlam saw the making of WWE history with the unveiling of the WWE Universal title. The unveiling made for the first reveal of a brand-only title for *Raw* since the World Heavyweight Championship in 2002.